Food

Kay Davies
and
Wendy Oldfield

641.3 (4)

Wayland

Starting Science

Books in the series

Animals
Electricity and Magnetism
Floating and Sinking
Food
Information Technology

Light
Skeletons and Movement
Sound and Music
Waste
Weather

About this book

Focusing on foods that children will be familiar with, this book introduces them to the importance of eating a balanced diet. Through observation and recording activities, it compares our eating habits with those of other animals, and looks at where foods come from and how they are made. It encourages children to think about ways in which foods are stored and labelled, and how water is essential for life.

Food provides an introduction to methods in scientific enquiry and recording. The investigations are designed to be straightforward but fun, and flexible according to the abilities of the children. The main picture and its commentary may be taken as an introduction to the topic or as a focal point for further discussion. Each chapter can form a basis for extended topic work.

Teachers will find that in using this book, they are reinforcing the other core subjects of language and mathematics. Through its topic approach *Food* covers aspects of the National Science Curriculum for key stage 1 (levels 1 to 3), for the following Attainment Targets: Exploration of science (AT 1), The variety of life (AT 2), Processes of life (AT 3), Types and uses of materials (AT 6), and Energy (AT 13).

First published in 1990 by
Wayland (Publishers) Ltd
61 Western Road, Hove
East Sussex, BN3 1JD, England

© Copyright 1990 Wayland (Publishers) Ltd

Typeset by Nicola Taylor, Wayland
Printed in Italy by
Rotolito Lombarda S.p.A., Milan
Bound in Belgium by Casterman S.A.

British Library Cataloguing in Publication Data
Davies, Kay 1946–
Food
1. Food
I. Title II. Oldfield, Wendy III. Series
641.3

ISBN 1 85210 995 5

Editor: Cally Chambers

CONTENTS

MOTHER'S MILK

When some animals are born, they feed on their mothers' milk.

Animals that do this are called mammals. Mammals usually have hair and are warm-blooded.

People are mammals too.

Which of these babies are mammals?

Milk is a good food for all baby mammals. It helps them to grow and to have strong teeth and bones.

As people grow older, milk is still a good food for them.

We drink the milk from cows, sheep and goats.

We can also use their milk to make butter, yoghurt and all kinds of cheese.

4

The young calf drinks its mother's milk.
When it gets older it will eat grass instead.

It is fun to eat a picnic outside in the summer.
We like to have different foods to choose from.

IT DOES YOU GOOD

We have to eat different kinds of food to help us grow and keep healthy.

There are body-building foods like meat, fish, eggs, cheese and beans.

We need vegetables and fruit which grow on plants and trees.

Some foods, like bread, potatoes and cakes, give us lots of energy.

A meal of fish, chips and carrots, then apple pie and custard, gives us all the sorts of food we need.

Choose a meal that you like to eat.
Draw a chart like this.

Is there a food in each column?

Does your meal have everything needed to keep you healthy?

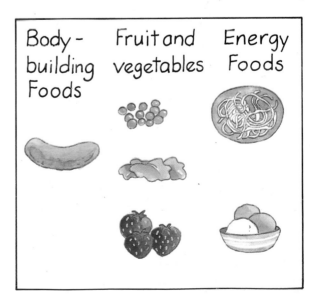

OUR DAILY BREAD

We grow some kinds of grasses to harvest their seeds or grains. We call these cereal crops.

Grains like wheat are ground up to make flour.

All kinds of bread can be made from flour.

Loaves of bread are made in all shapes.

To make flour into bread, it is mixed with other ingredients like water, sugar, salt, fat and yeast.

Yeast is a kind of fungus which makes a gas as it grows. The bubbles of gas make the bread swell up.

Put some yeast in a bottle with sugar and warm water.

Fit a balloon over the top and leave it in a warm place.

Watch the gas blow your balloon up.

The machine cuts the wheat. It removes the stalks and husks. The grains are collected to be used for food.

Eating fresh vegetables keeps us healthy. Sometimes we can harvest really fresh vegetables from the garden.

VEGETABLE STEW

Vegetables are parts of plants that are good for us to eat. We can cook them or eat them raw.

They may be the roots, stalks, leaves, flowers or seeds of a plant.

Carrots grow under the ground. They are swollen roots.

Celery is a long leafstalk that grows out of the ground.

Cabbage leaves grow in a tight ball from the stem of the plant.

The flower of a cauliflower grows in a ring of leaves.

Peas are the seeds of a plant. They grow inside long pods.

Can you think of some vegetables that you like to eat? Which part of the plant do they come from?

The fruits come from countries around the world.
Which ones do you recognize on this fruit stall?

FRUIT SALAD

Fruits grow on trees, bushes and other plants. They are the ripe, swollen bases of flowers that have died.

Seeds grow inside a fruit.

If the fruit falls to the ground a new plant may grow from the seed.

Ask an adult to cut up some fruits.

Can you find the seeds inside?

Some fruits, like apples, are sweet and taste good raw. Others, like lemons and limes, are really sour.

Find lots of fruits. Look at them and taste them. Make a record of what you find in a chart like this.

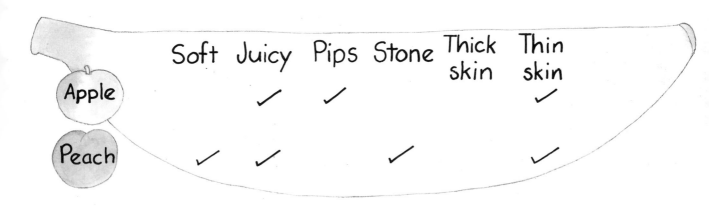

	Soft	Juicy	Pips	Stone	Thick skin	Thin skin
Apple		✓	✓			✓
Peach	✓	✓		✓		✓

MEAT PIE

Some animals hunt and kill other creatures for food.

Animals that eat meat have long, pointed teeth called canines.

These teeth are perfect for biting and tearing meat into pieces.

Which are the meat-eaters here?

People also eat meat and have canine teeth.

But we buy our meat and cook it to make it soft.

Sometimes we cut it up with a knife and fork.

We don't have to use our canine teeth as much as animals do.

14

The meat is being cooked on a barbecue. This makes the meat easy to chew. It looks and smells good.

A FISH DISH

Eating the flesh of fish and other animals makes you grow. It helps to mend your body if it is damaged.

Fish are caught from the seas and rivers of the world.

We eat fish like cod, herring and trout.

Shellfish like mussels and crabs have hard shells. The tasty flesh is inside.

You can make a frying pan to fry a fish dish.

Find a paper plate. Cut a handle out of thick card. Stick it in place and paint your frying pan.

Paint some fish and cut them out. Pretend to fry them in your pan and serve them on a plate.

What else would you like to cook with your fish?

The fishermen send their catch to market straight away.
People want to buy fish when it is still very fresh.

These colourful pulses will have to soak up water and be cooked before they can be eaten.

FEELING THE PULSE

Some people do not eat the flesh of fish or animals. They are called vegetarians.

But they may eat the foods that come from living animals, like eggs, milk, butter and cheese.

These people have to make sure that they eat enough of other body-building foods.

They can eat nuts, beans and lentils. These are all the seeds of plants.

Some seeds which have been dried are called pulses.

Collect different pulses.

Find out their names.
Feel them.

Soak some in water overnight.
Do they change shape?
Do they feel the same?

Plant a few soaked pulses in some soil.

Do any grow into plants?

KEEPING FRESH

The foods that we store must be kept safe to eat.

The air around us is always full of tiny germs and moulds that we cannot see.

They use our food to grow and live on. They can make us very ill.

There are lots of ways to stop our food going bad.

Can you match up these foods with how they have been stored?

Butter   Biscuits   Baked beans   Jam

Cornflakes   Sugar   Lemonade

A   B   C   D

E   F   G

Foods can be kept cool in the fridge, or frozen in the freezer.

Tins, jars, bottles, boxes, paper bags and plastic wraps can seal out all the air with germs and mould.

We can store foods with lots of vinegar, sugar or salt. Germs don't like food that is too sour, sugary or salty.

At the factory the vegetables are put into glass jars.
The lids are put on very tightly to keep the air out.

We can't always see what is in tins and boxes.
The labels tell us about the food or drink inside.

LOOKING AT LABELS

Labels tell us which country the food comes from and what is inside. They tell us if there are extra things added, like sugar or salt.

Tins and boxes have big labels and pictures, to tell us what is inside.

Jars and bottles have small labels. We can see what is inside.

Eggs and bananas don't need labels. We know what they are.

Make a shop on the wall.

Stick sheets of plain paper on a wall.

Collect food labels or make your own.

Paste them on to your shop on the wall.

FOOD FOR ALL

Some creatures eat plants. Some eat meat.

Others, like ourselves, can eat both.

Every creature on earth fits into a pattern called a food chain. Food chains always begin with a plant.

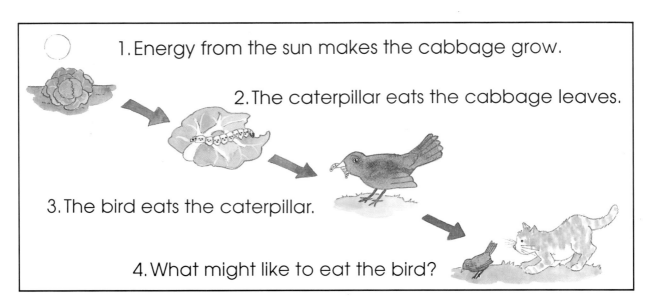

1. Energy from the sun makes the cabbage grow.

2. The caterpillar eats the cabbage leaves.

3. The bird eats the caterpillar.

4. What might like to eat the bird?

Make some food chains of your own.

How many creatures can you fit into your chain?

Don't forget, there are food chains in ponds, rivers and seas too.

The wildebeests would like to stop and eat the grass.
But they have to keep running away from the lions.
The lions would like to eat the wildebeests.

The giraffe and zebras live where it is hot and dry.
They come to the water-hole to drink.

WATER FOR LIFE

Every living thing must have water.
Animals drink water, and plants need it to grow.

When there is no rain for a long time, people cannot grow crops or keep animals.

They may die because they have nothing to eat.

You can grow your own crop of cress like this.

Find two jars.

Cover them with plain paper and paint the faces of Bald Bobby and Hairy Henry.

Fill them both with newspaper scraps and put a layer of cotton wool on the top.

Soak Henry's jar with water and then sprinkle cress seeds in both.

Wait for a few days to see Henry's hair grow.
Why do you think Bald Bobby's hair did not grow?

MY FAVOURITE FOOD

Like us, some animals eat many sorts of food. They have their favourites too.

The dormouse will eat berries but likes hazelnuts best.

The thrush eats insects and seeds but prefers fat snails.

What is your favourite food?

Ask your friends what they like to eat best. Make a block graph like this to show everyone's favourite foods.

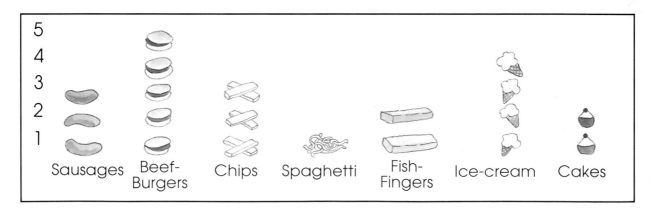

Look at your block graph. Which food do most people like best? Which food do least people like best?

The party food is in lots of dishes.
We can choose our favourite foods to eat.

GLOSSARY

Calf   A baby cow.
Canine teeth   Long pointed teeth used for tearing and biting meat.
Cereal crops   Grasses like wheat, oats and rye, whose seeds are used for food.
Cress   A plant with tiny green leaves. It is eaten in salads and sandwiches.
Crops   Plants that are grown for food.
Energy   Something we have to have, in order to do anything at all.
Flesh   The part of an animal's body that covers the bones.
Food chain   A pattern that shows what animals eat and what they are eaten by.
Fungus   A living growth which prefers damp places. It is not an animal or a plant.

Germs   Tiny forms of life that can sometimes make us ill.
Grains   The seeds of grasses.
Harvest   To gather or pick crops.
Husks   The tough, dry cases of grains.
Ingredients   The things that are mixed together to make a food.
Lentils   Small round seeds of a plant, rather like peas.
Mould   A furry fungus that can grow on food.
Pulses   The seeds of peas, beans or lentils, that we can eat.
Stem   The stalk of a plant.
Vegetarians   People who do not eat the flesh of animals.

FINDING OUT MORE

Books to read:

Dairy Cows by Cliff Moon (Wayland, 1983)
Finger Foods by Chris Deshpande (A & C Black, 1988)
Food by Beverly Mathias and Ruth Thomson (Franklin Watts, 1989)
Food by Ruth Thomson (Franklin Watts, 1989)
Harvest Festival by Renu Nagrath Woodbridge & Lynne Hannington
   (A & C Black, 1988)
Health and Food by Dorothy Baldwin (Wayland, 1987)
Healthy Eating by Wayne Jackman (Wayland, 1990)
My Apple by Kay Davies and Wendy Oldfield (A & C Black, 1990)
My Class Enjoys Cooking by Ruth Thomson (Franklin Watts, 1986)
My Visit to the Supermarket by Diana Bentley (Wayland, 1989)
Stir-fry by Renu Nagrath Woodbridge (A & C Black, 1989)
Taste by Wayne Jackman (Wayland, 1989)
Tasting by Henry Pluckrose (Franklin Watts, 1987)
What's that Taste? by Kate Petty (Franklin Watts, 1987)

The following series may also be useful:

Food (Wayland)
Let's Visit a Farm by Sarah Doughty and Diana Bentley (Wayland)

PICTURE ACKNOWLEDGEMENTS

Bruce Coleman Ltd. 25 (Ziesler), 26 (Cubitt); Eye Ubiquitous 17; Hutchison 12; PHOTRI 9, 10, 20; Topham 5; Wayland Picture Library 4, 16 top, the following commissioned from Chapel Studios (Zul Mukhida) cover, 8 bottom, 13, 14, 16 bottom, 19, 23, 24, 27, 29; ZEFA 6, 8 top, 15, 18, 21, 22.
Artwork illustrations by Rebecca Archer.
The publishers would also like to thank Davigdor Infants' School, Hove, St Bernadette's First & Middle School and Downs County First School, Brighton, East Sussex, for their kind co-operation.

INDEX

Page numbers in **bold** indicate subjects shown in pictures, but not mentioned in the text on those pages.